the

leaving

camille yameen

the leaving copyright 2019 © by Camille Yameen.

All rights reserved. Printed in the United States of America.
No part of this book may be used or reproduced in any form or by any means without permission, except in the brief case of quotations in critical reviews.

First printing 2019

ISBN 9781792788697

Cover art copyright 2019 © by Ryan Marquardt

Editing by Ryan Marquardt
Artistic direction by Ryan Marquardt

www.camilleyameen.com

for the ones who leave:

i want to take a moment
to kiss your eyelids
to hug your elbows
to tell you
i know
i know
i know
that decision was not easy
i know
it was the most
difficult
and treacherous
impossible
thing
and
really
you had only
two
choices
one
slowly poison yourself
until you disintegrate completely or
two
rip out your guts

camille yameen

the leaving

contents

i..1

ii..83

iii..189

glossary of things...255

there is nothing for me here
i decided
it is only crumbs and dirt
so i slipped on my wings
like a backpack
gorged on insects and grain
and wiped
the
violet berry
juice
dribbling
down
my
chin
and i went

-prologue

i.

camille yameen

the leaving

how can they both be true? he begs
tears rush from his eyes like traffic
like hostages he's kept captive his whole life
like he's never taken a breath

*how can you say you love me
but want to leave at the same time?*

i tell him

there can be
more than one truth
it is not mutually exclusive

> *i am tired and i don't want to go to bed
> it is cold outside and the sun is shining
> i love you and i am unhappy*

see - they are all true things

i watch him wilt in front of me

camille yameen

it hurts differently than i imagined
i always thought it would feel like
    torture like
    inside out contact lenses like
    funny bone throbbing like
    third degree burns like
    a gunshot like
    biting my tongue like
    waking up during surgery like
    a papercut like
    bleeding out like
    a hangnail

                                  it is worse.

-the leaving

the leaving

here
i said
sending my hands
giftwrapped for you
emptiness doesn't suit them

this
you can have
offering my liver
sliced fresh from my abdomen

wear them like a necklace
my vocal cords
pulled from my neck like puddy
i have nothing to say

and this
ripped from its cage
my heart
seizing and bloody
just go.
i have no use for it anymore.

camille yameen

while you slept last night, i laid next to you.

while you slept last night, i laid next to you in the dark.

while you slept last night, i laid next to you in the dark and cried.

while you slept last night, i laid next to you in the dark and cried and cried and cried and cried.

-i leak what i cannot say

the leaving

does anyone cry gently?
i have never.
      not even once.
wept quietly
even in the moments
when no noise was made
i could still hear my sternum
bending
cracking
a tree trunk snapping
vicious
        slanted
hurricane rains
collapsed lungs into rubble.

the shredding
of land.

camille yameen

you pick yourself up
like you are a newborn animal
or a boulder.
you are flimsy
but heavy.
is it possible to find footing
and to be the footing?
is it possible
to be the thing that walks
and the thing that remains?
can it be
that you
must move
but don't yet know how?
for up until this exact moment
you have never needed yourself.
what does it feel like
to know for certain
that you
are again new and because of that
you
are the most precious piece of the universe.

the leaving

who do you think you are
he asks
we fly in circles like this
questions
my whole life has been a question
that doesn't have any answers
answers
that don't belong to any question
it's a cruel game
i played
even before i learned to blink
what did i do
he questions
maybe
i tell him
maybe
this is not even about you

camille yameen

we were
convenient
for each other
like sweatpants
like keeping your shoes tied
like plastic bags
like calling in sick
like staying

-that is not love

the leaving

when it all explodes around you
do not take cover
do not run from the shrapnel
do not dodge the noise
stand as tall as you can
stretch your ribs across the world
open them like a mouth
let the crown on your head
glisten against the gunfire
because
among the bullets
chopping the invisible air
are your skin cells
and your molecules
you are a piece of this
in a way no one else
is a piece of this
and you belong
among the shrapnel
among the noise
you have a place in things unsettled
and unpeaceful
you belong to this chaos
and it belongs
to you

camille yameen

i watch the news
the bombings
the raids
the killings
the massacres
in the land
and inside myself
my land
i am a piece of
but am not a whole of
it is no wonder
things happening there
are also happening inside of me
it is no wonder
i know nothing
it is a stubborn
helpless
empty disconnection
of where i am
with who i am

-privilege

the leaving

i am not muslim
i tell them
when they ask if i celebrate christmas
if that's what you're asking
they tell me that's not
what
they're
asking
but i can smell it on their lies
like garlic

camille yameen

it feels
the way it feels
when you pierce your ears
quick
deceivingly painless
    at first
sharp and
tender
you sleep on your back
uncomfortable
adjust
swollen
then the throbbing
followed
by
the incessant ache

the leaving

i woke to shards
of glass
piercing the ground
like olympic javelins
splinters twisted
between branches
above me
a hole
hangs open like a jaw
jagged
vampiric
black and violent
it's not a shattered ceiling
it's a broken sky

there is something that happens to you
the first time your heart breaks
you become a member
elite
of a club you never knew existed
people see you
and they can feel
just as you can feel

something
is different

-baptism

the leaving

but what was it like
i ask my arab grandfather
of the place my feet
have never walked
but his remain rooted
i am starving
for
the breadcrumbs to his past
he drowns a slice of lemon in his tea
with a spoon
it rises to the top
like the sun
it was
heartache and home.

camille yameen

can you mourn a place
you've never been?

-a question of ancestry

the leaving

i taste the
sorrow
when it crawls down my cheeks
and over my lips
like a spider
it is a bitter longing
that
never leaves

camille yameen

there is a special kind of hollow
reserved for the people
and places
that leave
it lives
inside you
or in the people
or places
you left
when they decide
or you decide
their place
or your place
is no longer among you
or them
the hollow expands like a balloon
in the belly of the thing
and they
and you
and we
are never again the same.

the leaving

perhaps
if i fill myself with men
then
then
yes then
i will be full
(it is a hunger, too, you know
like bingeing on junk food
but i know
in an hour
i will be starving)

again.

camille yameen

they came for me.
the men.
one after another
like vultures.
ripped from me
what they desired
and lusted after.
ravenous
scavengers
shredded me raw
like cabbage
gouged my eyes
with blood-soaked beaks
they arched their backs
and grunted in celebration
as they feasted.

they came for the carcass.

and left only the bones.

the leaving

sometimes i wonder
    do you know these poems are about you
but when i feel the next one
seep out of my skin
i think
    how can you not?

camille yameen

i am always losing things

one sock

bobby pins

my train of thought

car keys

receipts

hair ties

you

the leaving

do you think
when the first stem
sprung up from the earth
gasping and
in search of the light
the ground screamed in agony
convinced
something horrific was happening
do you think
it cried out in pain
as it broke itself apart
certain it would never heal
do you think
we are the same?

camille yameen

there was a time
a brief time
that was not so brief
when even the sun
didn't want me anymore
you
the sun said
are sucking the life
and the light
out of me.

-sadness

the leaving

every morning i pick up the pieces
and tape them
carefully
back
where
they
are
supposed
to be
chipped edges
hold on for dear life
loose
but we are in it together
then
you call my name
and i burst at the seams

-i fall apart

camille yameen

i am part gypsy
a wild
vagabond
thief
of hearts.
give me your hand
to lick the lines on your palm
inhale you like cologne
then help
me
tie bells around my ankles
and watch
me dance
in circles
don't blink
i'll be gone before you know it

-we all leave differently

the leaving

as if i am removing
a fish hook
from his cheek
i release him
from me

-mercy

camille yameen

i
i am
i am not
i am not enough
i am not dark enough
i am not light enough
i am not white enough
i am not enough
i am not
i am not enough of anything

-for you or for me

the leaving

lay flat
i threaten
my curls
to obey
frizzy and rebellious
i stand for hours in front of a mirror
until my arms throb
heavy
like stones
i will fry the life out of them
i will burn them straight

camille yameen

growing up in my house
being arab
was something seen but hardly spoken of
it was the expensive antique knife on the shelf
and the *ful medames* on the table
but not the conversation surrounding it
it was the rug pressed against the bottom of my feet
but never the land beneath them
it was the click of the clock
with arabic numbers hanging in the bathroom
but never the right time to discuss it
it was the scarf around my father's neck
and the questions trapped in mine

-stuck

the leaving

so what are you
people ask me
as if the answer should be easy
i should be used to it by now
but i'm not
i will never get used to
the feeling
of people wondering
what
not who
i am

camille yameen

in the middle of the night
my tree branch
limbs
were aching for you
every inch of me
sore
and when outstretched arms
returned empty
the feeling of
your absence
was the same
as when you keep climbing
and think
there is
an extra

                                        stair

the leaving

walking up and down
the aisles at my grandfather's middle eastern grocery store
there are too many foods i cannot pronounce
and spices i do not know how to use

-imposter

camille yameen

i have been envious of my father
my entire life
and he has no idea
the jealousy i felt
for what his eyes have consumed
my mouth is a desert
dried and callused
from the times i swallowed my admiration
instead of speaking it
for all the moments i could've filled the quiet
by asking for stories
of his life before i was a spark in the sky
but didn't
i chose not to
and instead
i buried my neck in the mud
i hid in the shadow of the tree

the leaving

one summer at the pool
a young child pointed to my brother and me
splashing
then turned to our mother
and asked
are those little brown children yours?

that was the beginning of the uncertainty of my belonging

camille yameen

little light skinned girl
next to her bigger browner skinned brother
why can't i look like you
she asks
with electrocuted curls
no one thinks i belong to us

-the difference of pigment between siblings

the leaving

my parents always reminded me
to wish our family a happy *ramadan*

and i did
but i always forgot to ask

what does it all mean? and

how do you believe in what you cannot see? and

do you feel abandoned? and

where do you place your hands? and

how have you memorized so many so many so many words? and

what does praying taste like? and

does it feel like spring? or

does it smell like winter? and

how do you know if allah hears you? and

if i had been born in another life, would i be celebrating, too?

this morning
i searched everywhere for my car keys
    in the ocean depths of purses
    pockets of unwashed jeans
    the fridge
exhausted i gave up
it was as if they had evaporated
hours later
i found them
    naked
    alone
    and frightened
please they pleaded through vibrating teeth
please
stop forgetting
where you
place
me

the leaving

everyone is our teacher
my mother said
holding me against her chest
again
like again
i was a child
as i collapsed beneath a broken heart
again

camille yameen

everything is not easy.
everything is not.
everything is.
everything is.
everything is.
everything is everything is everything is everything is everything is
everything is everything is everything is everything is everything is
everything.

the leaving

i know the empty

hurts

but

sometimes

the emptiest things

are the most

remarkable.

have you seen

the grand canyon?

-peace

camille yameen

he is not worthy of you
he is not worthy of you
he is not worthy of you
he is not worthy of you
he is not worthy of you
he is not worthy of you
he is not worthy of you
he is not worthy of you

the leaving

it shouldn't be a contest of
whose pain is greater
but it is
we compare horror and
carry it over our arms
like a new purse
oh, this old thing?
let me tell you of the time
i didn't get out of bed for a week
or the time
i drank myself into the darkness
or the time
i tore all the paper from the walls
let me tell you of the time
i didn't think i'd come back
they should give medals
for the wars we survive
between our bones
the ones where we are the enemy
and the casualty
and the hero
they should give medals to wear
so we would know, without having to rip off the scab,
what we have each been through

-compassion

camille yameen

and so
his words will skin you
like a deer
when you leave him
they will expose you
inside out
and
raw
naked in a way you
have never been
it is agony
but it is not eternity

the leaving

you came home and saw
i had broken every mirror in the house
why did you do this?
you asked as you swept the pieces
because
i said
i cannot stand to look at her any longer
you said
who?
i said
me

camille yameen

we loved

as if he was fragile

and dangerous

like cracked glass

or dry ice

we loved

as if i was weak

and transparent

like lemon water

or smoke

the leaving

it only aches a little
but like careful steps
on antique floors
it can't be unheard.
the call from underneath.
the squeal from too much
pressure.
release the boot
and the floor
gasps for air.
like i am
the hardwood
and you are
sole.

camille yameen

you thought him a god
he was mere mortal

the leaving

some nights
i stack pillows on your side of the bed
press them against my spine
and pretend you're still there

some nights
i stack pillows on your side of the bed
press them against my stomach
and pretend i'm still there

some nights
i stack pillows in the bathtub
press my skin against the cool porcelain
and pretend

camille yameen

pretending to teach
the substitute
pauses
when she gets to your name
and weak smiles
embarrassed
and up looks
nervous

you know she is waiting
for someone to speak up
and save her
like you have
always waited for someone to save you
in that moment

ummm
she says
the class giggles and
you raise your hand

the leaving

maybe if you

held your breath
until your lungs dried and crumbled like leaves
tied your palm
to the stove
sliced open your skin
with a grapefruit spoon
sanded your sharp edges
with silk

maybe you, too,
would know it feels like
to care for you

camille yameen

some people's souls have chosen to suffer in this lifetime

-you cannot save them

the leaving

it's the same feeling after running a marathon
i think
like two hours of sleep
like late night heavy eyelids
like outside all day in the heat
like dodging rain
like constant creativity
like grief

it's just.
exhausting.

-the missing

camille yameen

and anyway
he didn't believe in your magic

the leaving

but where
do birds go
during storms?

-humans, too?

camille yameen

i found a turtle in the middle of the road
smashed by the wheels of a car
i shook so hard
at her death
i did not even recognize the wails
as they escaped my mouth

the leaving

i sit and wait
for the grief to retract
its claws
back into the sea

camille yameen

there is a poem

trapped

in the undertow
of my tongue
it is drowning
stuck
    lodged between
    everything i've told you
    and everything i still want to say
it is suffocating me

the leaving

we were supposed to go
when i was 18
but summer jobs and summer boys
and i didn't have time

we were supposed to go
when i was 22
but graduation and new jobs
and i didn't have time

we were supposed to go
when i was 26
but i had just returned from abroad
and i didn't have time

we are supposed to go
in this life
but the air is running out

-palestine

when you get into his car
so he can drive you home
in the morning
you notice something you didn't the night before

a car seat

and then you know

so you say
that's a nice car seat
and
did your wife pick it out
and he says
thank you
and
yes

you have never hated yourself more

when you arrive home
you throw up

when you look in the mirror
you do not recognize yourself

overnight you have transformed into a wolf
a creature that knows
no one is safe

the leaving

i sit shaking
head
cradled
in my hands like the world
fingertips bloody
over the keyboard
the words
i weep
they are still so empty

camille yameen

forgive me.
for my hands
smeared tacky in glue and
wood chips
the tape
webbed between my fingers
there is not a space
not one single space
left.
forgive me.

i am simply trying
to hold
everything
together.

the leaving

you can't take them with you

camille yameen

things leave
and things stay
the difficulty is figuring out
which is which

the leaving

i have fallen in lust so many times
stuck my fist in my mouth
and thought it love
i have given myself to men
who only gave me their evenings
i have left tiny pieces of myself
wedged in the cracks of their apartments
smeared on bathroom counters
and stuffed between the pages of a book
evidence
that once
i was there
he'll find it when he least expects it
maybe he has almost forgotten me
but when he does
find it
and
he remembers
i
will go running back

camille yameen

my father caught me staring at a globe when i was young
eyes squinted and clenched tight enough
to see the galaxies under my eyelids
my little bird hands spread as big as they could go
digging
sharp blue paint chipped and hidden
under my fingernails

i still carry it with me

the leaving

my jaw is full
of cotton balls
and razorblades
nothing comes out right
i swallow mouthfuls of blood
and choke
on all the things
no one seems to understand

look

i said, eyelashes pointed to the sun

what?

he said, cocked chin confused

it is my love for you

i told him

but it hurts

he said

>i swallow the lightning storm
>brewing like coffee behind my teeth
>and turn my back to his eyes

i know

the leaving

i once drew a map
behind your kneecap
and admired the way
your veins resembled hurricanes
before they strike land
like a moment of absolution
before confessing sins
we charted destinations
to the places we'd only read
about in history books
--landlocked, we were
continents
two strong, sturdy masses
separated by an ocean of riddles
zigzagged shorelines
chipped curves of desperation
we stole pieces of one another
in the night
yanked each other
apart, jealous

left only with memories
that once upon a time in a faraway land
we were made for each other

-pangea

i wrapped my arms around mother earth
cradled her head in my lap
there, there, why are you crying?

i cannot find them anywhere.
she wept
what have you lost?
i asked her

humanity. i've lost them all.

the leaving

am i running from
or am i running to

-wisdom from my father

camille yameen

i will blame it on the seasons
the winds of change
and an uninhabitable home
the forest fires
that wring the oxygen from lungs
like a towel
i will blame it on the beasts
who roam in the night
i will blame it on others
that i was a follower
i will blame it on forgetting
that these things happen

but the truth is
i couldn't stay
and
i knew this was coming
all along

-instinct

the leaving

i melt into
the rug
on the living room floor
it is an heirloom
it is a gift
from my grandfather
i am trying to become small enough
to walk the maze of silk fibers
like a labyrinth

-maybe then i will understand

camille yameen

it's not that i fly on purpose
it's just
the natural
progression
of
things

-for birds especially

the leaving

for some reason
everyone else
decided
it was not important
for me
and my brother
to learn arabic
as children.
still.
and now.
why can't
we all
go back.

camille yameen

in case no one has told you
i want you to know
you cannot find new places or people
unless you leave the old ones

-migration

the leaving

oh, icarus,
    i wept
    kneeling
    cradling your head against
    my tender thighs
    enveloping you
like wings
    hands drenched in
    melted wax
        what have you done?

camille yameen

in case you forgot
you didn't ask me to stay

the leaving

maybe i will return to you
or maybe i won't

but first
i will return to me

camille yameen

ii.

camille yameen

the leaving

                                                  i repeat it
                             like i'm laying intricate
                         black and white mosaic tile
                                  in the bathroom
like fresh coats of watery cream colored paint
                                 over scuffed walls
            like oil on hinges of upset cabinets
                     like dusted baseboards
                           like a new roof
                                       like
                                       like
                                       like
        like maybe i'll rebuild this house

imsorryimsorryimsorryimsorryimsorryimsorryimsorryimsorryi

camille yameen

i would rather
split my heart completely in two
tear it like ice
and shatter it like paper
until it is impossible to puzzle
back
together
than walk
zombie
silent
forever rotting
and punctured
just beneath the surface

-a choice in how to hurt and how to heal

the leaving

i watched a flock of birds fill power lines to their brim
so many
the middle was bowing
with heaviness
i imagined the weight of the lines
backfiring
to slingshot the birds
up into the air
and leave their skeletons
on the street
like confetti
and remembered
how oh so many times
i felt
just the same

camille yameen

some days
i am a chameleon
succumbing adaptation
appearance altering
to fit
and belong everywhere

-or does it mean i belong nowhere

the leaving

the greatest loneliness
i have ever felt
in my entire life
is when i returned
to a world
that moved on
and didn't need me any longer

-time doesn't stop for anybody

camille yameen

at first
i am skeptical of him
like a conspiracy theory
but
like a conspiracy theory
i am intrigued
and cannot stop myself

the leaving

some days i am okay
other days i am not okay
and all of that
is okay

-okay?

when family visits from *the old country*
i am awkward.
glorious women in *hijabs*
sit on grey couches in
my parents' home
we hug and press foreheads together

    i try to absorb their language through osmosis

in the absence of conversation
we serve tea
quiet
except for the clink of spoons
against porcelain
i listen to their golden bracelets jingle
and the tongue of my grandfather as he translates

we sit respectful
nod
and tight-lipped smile
until the tea turns cold

-reunion

                              the leaving

hearing them speak
and not knowing what they are saying.

-envy

camille yameen

i used to think
write it
write it so you don't feel it anymore
now i know better
now i
write so all i do is feel

the leaving

the trouble
with
fighting the good fight
is

      everyone thinks
      they are

camille yameen

as hard as i try
i cannot get the recipes right
too much lemon
not enough garlic
sour *tahini*
bland
abandoned plates and broken meals
it'll be better next time
i apologize
to my hands
but
how can i know what i do not know because i do not know
what it is that i do not know until i know that i do not know it

-why didn't i ask for the recipes

the leaving

i thought love
would be the hardest thing to find
it wasn't.
compared to the rest
love is the easiest.
the hardest to find
is
belonging.

camille yameen

most mothers
braid their daughter's hair
secure it with delicate ribbons
and neon colored
elastic circles
but my mother couldn't
because my disobedient curls
unruly and thick
mocked her fingers
it was difficult to tame
then
in the fourth grade
i still had not properly mastered
how
to take care of my hair
so
i sat stiff in a salon chair
and
watched as a stylist
chopped
it
all
off

-it felt like losing a limb

the leaving

when you butcher my name
like a raw slab of meat
you tear apart
hundreds of years of history
inserting your arrogance like a knife
your lazy tongue
slides clumsy swollen around the letters
confused
and unforgiving
at how for once
something does not come easy for you

camille yameen

eating ribs.

finger-paints.

heartbreak.

baking cookies from scratch.

the truth.

identity.

children.

mud.

oil changes.

leaving.

staying.

it's all messy.

the leaving

the first one
hurts because you thought he was the love of your life

the second one
hurts because you swore you'd be more careful this time

the third one
hurts because you were sure he was different

the fourth one
hurts because you tried to keep it casual

the fifth one
hurts because you weren't enough for him

the sixth one
hurts because he wasn't enough for you

you stop keeping track after that
because there are too many to count. that is when you
start mending and stop looking for love in
someone else.

-heartbreak

rumman.
he tells me pointing to the red flesh in the bowls on the counter
it means pomegranate.

yes.
i say
but what will i do when you aren't here any longer?

-*jiddhi* (grandfather)

the leaving

it's too dangerous
was what i was told
when i asked to come along
to see for myself
it is not safe
for you

i tried to reason with them
but the lemon trees

but their voices covered me like fog

-buried alive

tell me
am i the villain in your story?
do you tell tales of the spells
i conjured while you dreamt
and love potions i forced
down
your
throat
do you paint me evil
and cunning
a wicked, wicked woman
does that make it easier for you?
tell me
am i the villain in your story?

the leaving

i will keep you warm
        the sun sings to me
i will be here for you
every morning
to remind you
where the goodness is

camille yameen

i search for answers in
my blood in
every papercut and
skinned knee i
do not know exactly what i
am looking for but i
think i
will know when i
see it

-DNA

the leaving

it's full of the souls
of
the brokenhearted men
i've left behind

-my hair

camille yameen

i would
hand my lover a needle and thread
demand *sew me back together*
i'd rip the seams open again

-how to make people stay

the leaving

i am grateful for you.
i cannot imagine
the pressure
you feel while
desperately
holding my ruptured
edges
in place
filling the gaps
spaces
between my wounds.
i cannot fathom
what it feels like
to exist between
pain

-to the glue that holds me together

my mother is made of sea glass and cinnamon
and is a master of seeing right through people
as if our skin is transparent
i have never been able to trick her
she knew my heart
before it was made
and she has known
what i have been searching for
before i began

the leaving

all they do is take
and take
and take
and take
and take
and take
and take
and take
and take
and take
and for once
i am giving back
to myself

camille yameen

i make a list
of all the things i want
but do not need
to make certain
i learn the difference between lust
and necessity
the difference between life
and death
a list of all the things to keep me alive
the things i cannot live without
i write and write and write
and down both columns
is only one word

you

the leaving

you have to decide
what is worth fighting about
and what is worth fighting for
and those are two very different things

camille yameen

it was
what
it was
and
it wasn't
what
it wasn't
and
that
is
the only thing we can know for certain

the leaving

i schedule lunches with my grandfather
at a restaurant he loves
he takes his own *pita* for us to share
because theirs is
too greek
he says
he speaks to the server in the language i do not know
but i do know
they are talking about me
the weather
the food
the other people in the restaurant
their wives
the hard times
he takes our order
    lentil soup
    shwarma
    labneh
    hot tea
and leaves
my grandfather and i talk about
me
the weather
the food
the other people in the restaurant
his wife
the hard times
then he pauses and
the air fills with nothing
but memories
of his childhood

camille yameen

i squeezed a light bulb
until it popped
until blood snaked down my wrist
like ivy
i soak in the embers
this
maybe this
will help me glow again

the leaving

the sequel is never as good as the original

-she's the generic version of me

camille yameen

nature's largest misconception
is the fragility of a twig
it is the foundation
for nests
that when woven together holds life
like a womb

the leaving

i am told
one day everything will all make sense
but i am not sure
when that day will arrive
or what
everything
is

camille yameen

tell me how much you miss it.

i ask my grandfather.

i cannot.

he says.

there are not enough words

in either language.

-bilingual

the leaving

you seem far away
he says
and you are
you are everywhere
but there
you have crawled into the depths
between your skin and your spine
he runs himself in circles
searching for you
come back
come back
come back

camille yameen

go
go
go
i tell myself
go back
to it
and stare it in the face
like it is your prey
do not be scared of what has already happened
it cannot hurt you again

the leaving

i swore
i would never need another man
they are unreliable
dangerous dragons
but
but
but
when he opened his mouth
i could hear a sparrow inside his throat

      singing

you must start simple.

wahid. one.

ithnan. two.

thalatha. three.

arba'a. four.

khamsa. five.

sitta. six.

sab'a. seven.

thamaniya. eight.

tis'a. nine.

'ashra. ten.

you must also start simple in love.

-they are not so different

the leaving

when i first saw you
flannel over your t-shirt
arms pretzeled
i couldn't stop imagining
our bodies
and instantly
i had to know what it felt like
to be that close to your skin

camille yameen

i cannot sleep
i toss under my covers
like i haven't eaten in days
weeks
ravenous
i cast spells over myself
wash with chamomile tea
rub basil on the soles of my feet
and wish you to me

the leaving

i love you like autumn

like color shifting gods and glorious hues
when you whisper my name like wind
i shake

i fall to the ground
in worship of you

camille yameen

do you think the mountains
are embarrassed of their height
when flirting with the rivers?
maybe that's what causes
avalanches
and rock slides.
the desperate longing to be held.

the leaving

the first time the sun saw the moon
it nearly took his breath away.
he'd spend hours perfecting his glow
in hopes she'd notice
and practiced the perfect opening line:
is it hot in here or is it just me?
but she didn't.
the brighter he shined
the harder she was to find.
on rare occasions, they'd be in the sky
together
but she wouldn't give him the time of day
except for half crescent winks
and then she'd disappear.
he loved her curves
and thought her craters exquisite
said he'd follow her to the ends of the earth
for the chance to tell her so.
he often felt like crying when he missed her
but the tears sizzled and evaporated
leaving only a steamy reminder
that he'd melt for her.
he went round and round
wondering if it was a waste of time to love her.
but still
he'd strain for her silhouette
over tie-dyed pastel clouds
glancing over his shoulder
hoping she'd be looking for him, too.

camille yameen

you can let your guard down
he says
and the room disintegrates around us
he is afraid i am preparing to fly away again
but i am afraid i am preparing to love him

the leaving

i'm a tangled mess of knots
twisted rope ends
golden and frayed
overhand and half stitch
figure eight and slip
unfinished
intimidating
square and sheet bend
i secure myself
to anything that holds
but he
unravels
me

camille yameen

they rise as if from
ashes of my skin
    the goosebumps
under his lips
a hundred
thousand
million maybe
tiny mountain ranges
    across my ribcage
fingertips
and wind exhales
    they rise

he reads me
like braille

with attribution to the poetry of tyler knott gregson

the leaving

the first time
you are with him
and you feel as if
you shed a skin
as he lays there
sleeping
know
that it is okay
that we must unbecome
before we become
and that
is the only way
to become whole

camille yameen

it is normal
to fight.
this and other things i know
to be true.
but. just because it is normal.
does not mean it is easy.
it still burns.
like baking soda and vinegar.
inside a science experiment volcano.

-erupt

the leaving

we don't say sorry
we make *sorry*
in our bed
over the couch
against the wall
on the floor
in the shower
we make *sorry* until we
forget why we needed to
say it in the first place

camille yameen

wear me like moonlight
like shadow explosions
firework remnants
and blush
bend me around your jaw
    curved
    broken and gentle
    woven between the gaps
    of your fingers
        they look so empty
    spill me over your kneecaps
i'll be soft, i swear
just
just take me with you
when you go

the leaving

your smile reaches across your face like
feathers floating in the air

camille yameen

is there any moment in history
in all of human existence
more lonely
than the moment
right after sex
the emptiness
could start a war

the leaving

i stopped believing in religion
after i realized
too many people swore
their way was better
and more right
than all the others
and people
and countries
and families
were
t o r n
a p a r t
like two halves of a peach

camille yameen

what will happen when you meet his family for the first time:

1. they will ask how to pronounce your name
2. then they will ask what it is
3. then they will nod softly like light
4. then they will say it is…interesting
5. then you will thank them
6. then you will take a drink
7. then they will clear their throats
8. then you will say how beautiful their home is
9. then they will relax
10. then you all will eat

-11. pass the bread, please

the leaving

it is not an easy thing
to heal
at first it is a gaping wound
    full of splinters
    and brick dust
then there is the pulling
the stretching
the itching
the creating
it is made from nothing
(the scar)
but fragments
    frayed edges
and hope

camille yameen

we're a hurricane
in the mornings
it must be the shaken wild hair
broken buildings
like twisted blankets
pillow casualties
sirens and elbow bent street signs
makeup stained
don't you remember
what it feels like
to be terrified
and excited
at the exact same time?

that's sort of what love is

the leaving

i wish
oh i wish
i had known my mother
when she was my age
i think
oh i think
we would have been friends

camille yameen

the most painful part of growing
is when the roots of a tree
begin to spread
like a fist opening to expose its palm
and begin to awaken the earth
they have to force the entire massive world
around them
to move
and make room
even though the ground
pushes back and
doesn't want to
but the roots
the roots know
something wonderful is about to happen

-birth

the leaving

a world without
my parents.
i do not think
i will survive it.

camille yameen

there are oh so many

types of missing

there is sorrow

there is indifference

there is anger

there is destruction

there is sleeplessness

there is hunger

and then

there is the way

i miss you

the leaving

the sheets
are full of stardust

your lips
taste
like the moon

i swear

i'll orbit you
until
the sun
burns out

camille yameen

apologies
are not something
she is particularly
good at
she's more of a
grand gesture
type
like surprise parties
like expensive dinners
like weekend getaways
so
the words
always felt small
like dust
unimportant and forgotten
maybe
she thought
maybe
i'll put it in a poem
instead

the leaving

the most earth-shattering thing
he's ever done
was the moment
right before he kissed me
the very first time
when he paused
and looked
and i looked
and he waited
and waited
and waited
and waited
and waited
and waited
and waited

camille yameen

the first time my eyes met his
all at once
my bones
glued themselves back together
look
they whispered
this one

the leaving

stay

i slip it between
700 thread count and memory foam
    casual
      like coffee
like the kind i want
so desperately
to make you in the morning

camille yameen

i offer myself to you
at the altar of my bed
fold your hands
    read me like scripture
    purposeful and proper
    memorize me like *hail mary full of grace*
take me like communion

-worship

the leaving

a belly full of laughter
is the most satisfying feeling
there is
hold on to me
please

camille yameen

some mornings he is the fiery clouds
some mornings he is the broken sunrise
i am always the inhale between

the leaving

tell me something poetic

he says to me

tell me something
you can only feel in your core
let it melt over your lips like lava
suffocate
and cover me like pompeii

i'm his mount vesuvius

camille yameen

i can't help but steal
pockets full
of
candy bars
kisses
thunder
blankets
glances
moments
the spotlight
i'm sorry
it's only so
i have more things
to give you

the leaving

i will climb him
like a mountain
over and over and over
again
give myself
over and over and over
again
and over and over and over
again
and over and over and over
again

-summit

i chase you like a high
as if pill smashing
and injections
can bring you to me
quickly

rush
        i'm consumed

i'd turn my skin inside out
give everything i am
sell everything i have

      jewelry
      watches
      old electronics
      dishes
      myself

just so you'll stick around
a little longer

-addict

the leaving

i used to run from the words
terrified of what they might mean
and what you would think
if you ever read them.

you know, we were going to move to saudi arabia
my mother told me of the dreams she and my father had
newly married, fresh like air, they planned to see the world
for years
they wanted to move through markets hand in hand
barter for spices and gold and fruit
but six weeks after they vowed themselves to one another
she found out she was pregnant
and a new baby
would make it difficult to fly across the world
make it difficult to live in a land unknown
so they scribbled their dreams on a notepad like a grocery list
and
tucked them into the middle drawer in the kitchen
maybe one day

-i think she wanted to be a bird, too

the leaving

why aren't you writing
he asks and i am
vulnerable
is it me?
he asks
the butterflies
fall from the sky of his neck
but what he doesn't see
gentle
is
he makes me write too much
too many
words
i can't make sense of
they are a kaleidoscope
shaken
jumbled mess of a language
i don't yet speak

-sometimes it is hard to put things into words and other times it is easy so please be patient with me

camille yameen

i know i
have loved you before
in a past life
i can feel it

-soul mates

the leaving

you're a thunderstorm
most people
are afraid to be caught in one
unprepared
but i live for them
the steady beating drum
of rain
windblown intensity
of belonging to something
i'd gladly take the power out
to sit in darkness
with you

camille yameen

i will build you
a kingdom
but i will not live inside
the walls with you
i can't
i will become
the moat

- i will surround and protect you

the leaving

i think when my grandfather crossed the ocean
he brought the whole thing with him
i can see it in his eyes
when he thinks no one is looking

camille yameen

when i see a woman sink her fangs into the flesh
of another woman
like a ripe piece of fruit
i want to run to the injured one
suck the poison out
and remind her of one thing

we are not all the same.

the leaving

it makes me violently sick
to think
of the girl you were with
before me
picturing you with her
is the closest to death i have ever felt
it is like
pulling out my veins
one
by
one
by
do you ever think of her
when i am with you?
or do you remember how she tastes?
why do i turn myself in horrid haunted circles
when all i want
is to love you better?

camille yameen

but when the twilight sky
covers his naked body
tangled not in sheets
but in half whispers
tucked inside your pillow case
he exhales rosemary
and

he is so beautiful

-what happens in the midnight hours

the leaving

he twirls my hair
and passes it
between his fingers
sorry
it's obnoxious
i say
tucking it behind my ear
apologizing
it is a phrase i use to excuse
the things i cannot control
he tugs lightly on one
rings it like a bell
no
he says
his lips press to my ear
it is perfect

camille yameen

you hate the phrase
make love
but tell me:
what else do you call
symphonies of piano fists pounding
on unsteady earths
musical vibrations
felt round the world
and numb hands
electrifying hues on
us
planets forever following
each other
and the ache
oh, the ache, of
when
i
can't
catch
my
breath

-semantics

the leaving

the words almost fall out.
somersaulting tumbling rock
    heavy
    and sure
a cascade of wanting
one slip
of lost footing
    and a plummet to the earth.

just wait.
the moment is coming.

-on not saying it (yet)

camille yameen

i'll hold your body like
a seatbelt
i'll swaddle you in bubble wrap
    surround you in
       packing peanuts
and *fragile* stickers.
you're safe here.

the leaving

i am sitting on the kitchen stool
at my parents' house
when my father tells me
he is taking a trip
the trip
of my dreams
with his father
my grandfather
because it might be the last one
and he
needs to see the family
i nod
and accept
the greatest disappointment of our kind
is that we believe
there will always be plenty of time
when in fact
time is a drought
sucking the ocean dry

camille yameen

i can't stop
dropping things
    a dinner plate
    a wine glass
    laundry baskets
    the phone
nothing sticks
only slips
right through
like sunlight through morning blinds
and weeds in asphalt
it's just
i'm not used
to holding onto
anything

the leaving

we must often demolish (smash)
things (shells)
in order to open them

walnuts

eggs

coconuts

oysters

hearts

don't you see
the goodness is what's inside
do not fear your brokenness

camille yameen

i will keep
keep
keep
keep
writing you poems
until my hands fall off
or my fingertips rot
or the earth collapses in on itself

-whatever comes first

the leaving

i hope you find some of you
in some of this
and think to yourself

finally. i am not alone.

-to the reader

camille yameen

sometimes i imagine my grandfather's life
in reverse.
his mustache fades from silver back to
jet black
and the wrinkles evaporate from his hands
and neck
like puddles.
his vision becomes clearer with every blink
his spine becomes straighter with every step
he stands tall
he becomes a man i have never known
i watch his life play backwards
until he becomes a boy again
chasing a dented soccer ball
through up-kicked dust clouds
down desert streets
like rewinding my favorite movie
so i can watch the characters with broken hearts
heal
and the hero return home.

it is a story
with the happiest ending.

the leaving

but how will i know

i ask my mother

you will know

she tells me

because you will look at him
you will see the rest of your life
and it will still not be long enough

when you stayed the first night
you didn't sleep a second
weeks later you told me

*i listened to you breathe
like i was hearing music
for the very first time*

you said

*and spent every moment wishing
that i could lay with you
for the rest of our lives*

the leaving

my grandfather came to this country
cradled to sleep
in the belly of a rocking
boat
when he was fourteen
with nothing
but tuberculosis
and no one
he was certain
he'd made a mistake
that he would die
alone
and with nothing
but tuberculosis

but he survived

-and so will i

camille yameen

tonight
the moon hung heavy
like a ripe mango
orange and
fluorescent
i was terrified it would drop
at any second
plunge to the earth
lay bruised
and worthless
splintered across pavement
and chunky gravel
i wondered who
would be the one to find it
cradle it
remind it
you're still useful

the leaving

my father is made of pine
and fire
he sang me lullabies about horses
when i was a child
and over dinner
he hands me a gold necklace with falcon talons
to wear around my neck
he says
you are my warrior for peace

a pillow
a map of palestine from the 1800s
a book of bedouin jewelry
keffiyeh
pictures of arabian costumes
a persian rug
a tapestry
his mother's hand sewn dress

-my grandfather has started gifting me items from his homeland because he doesn't want me to forget (and neither do i)

the leaving

we build what we can
with what we have
where we are
with who we are
and hope.
it is enough.

-humans are not so different from birds

camille yameen

i nurse my tired wings
each night with peppermint
and eucalyptus

cracked
bloody
and bandaged

that is how
i know i must be close to something

the leaving

the leaving

iii.

camille yameen

the leaving

i was never good at prayer
until my mother took my hand
and explained
god is a woman

flowers fell from her mouth
that
she said
is the secret to the universe

camille yameen

yameen
means at the right hand
means toward the right
means in the right direction
so
it is imprinted in my blood
that i am supposed to know where
i am meant to be
so
how strange
that for
so
much of my life
i searched in all the wrong places

-found

the leaving

barefoot
i stood
and buried my feet in soil
poured a bucket of water over my head
turned to the clouds
and opened my arms like a door
you yelled from the window
    what are you doing?
deeper
i sunk in my heels
cool earth
pressed between my toes
    staying grounded

-roots

camille yameen

hold yourself close
but hold your heritage closer
the smells from the stories
the lessons from the language
the yearning from the yellowing of the sun
and the flight
it took to get here

the leaving

your trendy food
was our baby food.
think about that
next time you
see a woman in a *hijab*
and scoff.

-the colonization of middle eastern cuisine

camille yameen

do not be afraid
of the holes
in your hands
or
the cracks
in your skin
or
the places
that are split
bent
and busted
that's where
the light
gets in

with attribution to the poetry of leonard cohen

the leaving

i forgive you
for the blood soaked words
plucked from your teeth
like a seed
and offered to me like a gift
it is not all your fault
you
forgot
there are more things
that make us similar
than keep us apart
i am not the scissors and you
are not the rock
we are both fragile and not fragile
like paper
and so
i will keep forgiving you
until you remember what love tastes like

-to the women who have been unkind to me

camille yameen

open yourself to love again.
it will be okay.

-this i know to be true

the leaving

i like to wake a few moments before him
pull the pads of my fingers gently down his chest
like toes dragging through sand
recount every freckle
just to make sure they are all still here
marvel
at the birds welcoming the daylight
i surrender to his warmth

camille yameen

i loved him until two in the morning
    the same way dandelions love
    sacrificing
    themselves
    on
    wishes
do they ever become whole again?
or do they find wholeness in disappearance?
maybe it isn't
so wrong
to lose yourself

        and then i loved him again

the leaving

some days are impossible
some days we rewind the words we've said
replay them
like a carousel
some days we tie ourselves in the knots
of our sweaters
some days we say
tomorrow
tomorrow with the prism sky, me too

camille yameen

of what brings you peace
of what is missing
of what completes you
of where you see yourself
of where you see your self
of where you take your heart
of where you belong
of what makes you whole
of what keeps you moving
of what makes your life interesting
of whatever it is

-the finding

the leaving

if i haven't heard from you
in hours
i am convinced you
are dead somewhere.
frantic
i check traffic reports
for accidents
to make sure
you aren't
being peeled off
the freeway
like a sticker.
i turn on the news expecting
shooters where you work.
call emergency rooms
asking for
someone matching
your description.
it's just.

i am sure.
that something will come.
and take you from me.

camille yameen

the words do not always come easy
they hibernate
like bears
like tulips
like bees

and remain still

-patience

the leaving

no matter
how much you love him
you must
remember
the
solar system is in
you

-do not forget yourself

camille yameen

i stopped thinking
a long
time ago
    and started feeling
    instead
like glass
like feathers
like silk
like skinned knees
like bruises
like crushed velvet
like warm

the leaving

oh no no no

those are not stretch marks

they are brush strokes

-masterpiece

i promise
to love you the same way
sugar loves coffee
and storms love wind
and roots thirst for rain
and if you ever forget
how much that is
try to remember:

it is the same way
lungs love
e x p a n d i n g

-as if there is no other option

the leaving

funny

when he looks at me
and i forget my own name
still

-on staying in love

camille yameen

i rise
covered in silver sky
in silky soft light
and
shhhhhhhhh

-let the morning come

the leaving

i want him
and wanting him
does not mean
i do not want me also

-you can have it all (and so can i)

camille yameen

she is made of
lavender
and smoke
and holds the planets
at the back of her throat.

she is not afraid.

of anything.

-girl

the leaving

the thing about words
is that sometimes
they are selfish
greedy
they take up too much
air
like a vacuum
    so please don't become red angry
    when
    i
    lay
    my
    finger
    across
    your lips
i just want
to breathe
with you
in the quiet

camille yameen

no matter what happens to you
no matter who happens to you
you must keep loving
yourself
with every ounce of your body
tether yourself to yourself
and never let go

-no matter what no matter what no matter what no matter what

the leaving

it seems as though
everyone has forgotten
our name
is not
human wretched
human rotten
human rage
human reprehensible
human miserable
human vile
our name
is
human kind

camille yameen

please
stop
destroying
each
other

-there is no prize for being the last one standing

the leaving

watching *pita bread* rise
is a miracle of its own kind

camille yameen

i pass a woman in a burka on the street.
my gaze sticks to her like syrup.
she can feel it.
but doesn't look up.
she's used to the gawking.
i'm sure.
but i don't stare at her because i think she's different.
i stare at her because i think we are the same.

the leaving

you don't have to be afraid
just gaze at the moon
a glowing sky body

just like yours

-comfort

camille yameen

women
always tell me
they are jealous
of my hair
i'd kill for curls like yours
they say
i
smile
and thank them
but behind clenched teeth
i grunt
i almost killed mine.

the leaving

did you know cicadas live underground up to seventeen years
ingesting root juice and sap
they bury themselves alive
and
when they are ready to face the outside
they shed their skin
abandoning who they once were
they molt
leaving under the pale full moon
a corpse
of who they used to be

camille yameen

my brother nicknamed me
medusa
because he said my hair looked like snakes

he nicknamed me
after a woman
who was once upon a time beautiful
the pursuit of many hungry men
but *poseidon* forced his way inside
raped her in *athena's* castle.
outraged
athena sought to punish *medusa*
for her wicked, wicked ways
transformed her luscious locks
into serpents
and cursed her face
so anyone who looked upon her
turned
to stone
medusa was beheaded.

my brother did not know that story
when he teased me for my hair
and nicknamed me after a woman
who was told the fault was hers.

how tragic
that for women
nothing has changed.

the leaving

i forgive myself
it is never too late
i am worthy

-rinse and repeat

camille yameen

he buries his face in my neck
his chin perfectly nestles into my collarbone
maybe this
this is what it feels like
to have a home

the leaving

i love scars
and knowing
i can be split
wide
open
gutted
exposed
turned
inside
out
and
still
my magical body
knows
how
to
glue
itself
back
to
gether
all
on
its
own

camille yameen

does the ocean
move
on purpose
or on accident?
does it mean to
wave
stretch
and seek
the shore
retreat and return?
always?
forever and
ever
and
ever
and
i do not know
but that is also how i love you

-natural

the leaving

hands of a clock
you can count on me
i'm steady
press my back against yours
hold our ground
you've got my twelve
i've got your six

-the only way we can fall asleep

camille yameen

when you touch me
it sets my skin on fire.
i smolder
and watch
charred fingerprints
appear like footprints
across sand.
indented.
it stings
and itches.
but baby,
i'd crumble
for you.

the leaving

birds fly in a v formation
with the strongest at the front
to carry the burden
and make it easier
on the rest of the flock
they sacrifice their wings
for the good of the journey
then
they rotate
turn taking
to arrive stronger
as one
and
that is our duty
to lessen the struggles
for those who come next

-we will rise

camille yameen

i was sorry for so long
because i stole your kneecaps
when you insisted on walking
you needed help
but i am not a doctor
so i simply set them next to you and ran
i heard
you have found love again
and so i hope
she bandages you in the ways
i never could

the leaving

you don't have to be the cool girl
the one you think he wants
the one who laughs at jokes aimed like spears at women
but glues her lips on politics
the one who drinks beer and never complains
when his eyes bounce around the room
the one who doesn't care that he won't hold your hand in public
and shrugs when he doesn't call you back
        even though you'll spend hours with your phone in your hand
        just in case
you don't have to be that girl
because
you will find someone
who understands you control the weather
and knows you carry the moon inside your mouth
someone who kisses you every moment he can
someone who knows you are a goddess
someone who will spend the rest of his life
making sure he deserves you

-letter to my younger self

camille yameen

if only you loved yourself
as hard as you loved him
my god
how full of love
you would be

the leaving

when we argue
we do not shout insults
or pull knives from our backs
we do not want to say things we will regret
instead
if we want to yell and
break dishes
we raise our voices
and with shaking pointing fingers scream

    i love you

    i'm not leaving you

    you mean everything to me

until our voices are raw
we replace passion with passion
and howl at the moon together

camille yameen

above all
keep breathing.
and in the silence
listen
let your lungs
remind you
of waves
of expands
of contrasts
of balance
of
and.
if you remember
one thing
and one thing
only

please remember

you will return
to yourself.

-the comeback

the leaving

hey you
yes, you
    with the crooked tooth
    and the worried lips
    and the train track heartbeat
be gentle
with yourself.

-also to the reader

camille yameen

i will not wake up tomorrow and understand
what it means to be arab
what it means to be woman
what it means to be
but maybe
i will wake up and understand
what it means to keep searching
and maybe the answer
is that there is no answer

-odyssey

the leaving

you must
say what it is
you want most
and until you do
it will never arrive

-speak it into existence

camille yameen

pull the thread
watch
as it all unravels around you
how glorious
it is
the unbecoming
of everything you thought
you were
supposed to be

the leaving

don't you see:

women shape our view
of the world
they mold it like clay

when we fight with friends
we are convinced
everyone
hates us

everyone
is out to get us

we are alone in the world

and when
our heart is trampled
we long for the company
of women
who understand

and when the world is right
women
women
women
are
the reason to celebrate

camille yameen

he says your name like it is a redwood
strong
and important
like it is natural
like you shatter walls of
sunlight
where you stand
like he can see your
intertwined roots
curling around the earth
sure of yourself
and unmoving
like he'll keep saying it for
centuries

the leaving

find the words
and chase them
until your lungs give out
and even then
keep chasing

camille yameen

i could write epic novels
of all the things i wish i told
my younger self
but i think
it all boils down to

the leaving

you can be both delicate
and dangerous

-fire

camille yameen

we are a
flock
of falcons
from the east

-family

the leaving

come with me
let's travel the world.
and then
let's build our own.

camille yameen

as i roll over
he asks where i came from
as if i couldn't possibly be from
anywhere he knows
i tell him
a bird's nest
i'm a mashup
(of sorts)
built from
twigs i've carried in my beak
caked thick in mud
crumbs of dry leaves
yarn
plastic bag splinters
i'm made up of everywhere
i've ever been.
he cups my cheek like water
pulls
from my hair
a
feather

the leaving

the sky opened up
and sighed

she split the clouds
like a wishbone

they curtseyed to the sun
and bowed to the wings

she is the great connector
of before and again and

after and there is nothing that makes her
beam quite like knowing

under her
all things come together

-i am also the sky

camille yameen

people always leave
but sometimes
they stay
and sometimes
we stay, too

the leaving

camille yameen

the leaving

you have roots
or
you have wings
and i
am a creature confused
for i
am continually fighting
for both
earth
and sky

-epilogue

camille yameen

the leaving

acknowledgements

this book would not be possible without you, the reader. thank you, from the deepest part of my soul for being here with me.

ryan, i cannot thank you enough for your vision. this became because of you.

my parents, linda and jamiel, thank you for giving me the words and the bravery. for allowing me to free bird my way around. you gave me the safest place to return, again and again.

thank you, drae. you are my heart.

and my *jiddhi,* thank you for everything.

camille yameen

the leaving

glossary of things

belonging: the thing we search for

bird: i am a bird, you are a bird, the one who left you is a bird, and so is the one who came back

circles: it repeats it repeats it repeats

family: our flock – sometimes we choose them, sometimes we don't

feathers: the things we leave behind

home: the thing we build, or try to

leaving: the thing we do when we can't stay

migration: the natural progression of things

mouth: where we hold all things true

staying: the thing we do when we don't leave

sun: you are the sun, i am the sun, and when we are not the sun, we are the moon

wings: the things that carry us

camille yameen

about the book

the leaving is a collection
it is an ode
a promise
a remembrance
a question
a sojourn
it is an earthquake and solid ground
it is about leaving
staying
searching
finding
losing
healing
becoming
and searching again
it is about the veins that run between them all.

camille yameen

about the poet

camille yameen is a palestinian-american publicist turned peace corps volunteer turned public speaker turned poet. she grew up near kansas city, missouri and studied communications at bradley university where she became a national champion in public speaking. she began her communications career in las vegas. after a while, she traded her office space for open countryside, red carpets for dirt roads, and ran away to africa to serve in the peace corps in madagascar. she came back to a world that was full and empty and confusing. so she traveled the country as a youth motivational speaker and presented before tens of thousands of students about leadership, bravery, and adventure. soon after, she dove back into communications, this time in the not-for-profit sector. all this time, she wrote. and wrote. and wrote. and wrote. and wrote.

the leaving is camille yameen's first book of poetry.

Made in the USA
Columbia, SC
22 July 2023